My First PRAYER and GRATITUDE JOURNAL

DAILY BLESSINGS AND BIBLE VERSES FOR KIDS

BY PIA IMPERIAL

ILLUSTRATED BY Risa Rodil

Grosset & Dunlap

GROSSET & DUNLAP
An imprint of Penguin Random House LLC, New York

First published in the United States of America by Grosset & Dunlap,
an imprint of Penguin Random House LLC, New York, 2024

GROSSET & DUNLAP is a registered trademark of
Penguin Random House LLC.

Visit us online at penguinrandomhouse.com.

Printed in India

ISBN 9780593750902   10 9 8 7 6 5 4

Design by Kimberley Sampson

This Journal Belongs to:

_____

Table of Contents

BIBLE VERSES

Strength Through Faith

Patience, Kindness, and Ambition

God's Love

Trust in Yourself

Overcoming Adversity

Prayers

Date: Su / M / Tu / W / Th / F / Sa
__ / __ / ____

Today I Feel:

😄 😊 😐 😔 😣

I am thankful for _____ because

_____

_____ .

Blessings the Day Has Brought:

1 _____

2 _____

3 _____

Bible Verse for the Day

But they that wait upon the Lord shall renew their strength; they shall mount up with wings as eagles; they shall run, and not be weary; and they shall walk, and not faint.—Isaiah 40:31

Date: Su / M / Tu / W / Th / F / Sa

__ / __ / ____

Today I Feel:

I am thankful for _____ because

_____

_____ .

Blessings the Day Has Brought:

1 _____

2 _____

3 _____

Moment of Reflection

What is something you want to thank God for today?

Date: Su / M / Tu / W / Th / F / Sa
__ / __ / ____

Today I Feel:

I am thankful for _____ because

_____

_____ .

Blessings the Day Has Brought:

1 _____
2 _____
3 _____

Bible Verse for the Day	When I am afraid, I will put my trust in you.—Psalms 56:3

Date: Su / M / Tu / W / Th / F / Sa

__ / __ / ____

Today I Feel:

I am thankful for _____ because

_____

_____ .

Blessings the Day Has Brought:

1 _____

2 _____

3 _____

Moment of Reflection

Write about a time when you trusted God.

Date: Su / M / Tu / W / Th / F / Sa
__ / __ / ____

Today I Feel:

I am thankful for _____ because

_____

_____ .

Blessings the Day Has Brought:

1 _____

2 _____

3 _____

Bible Verse for the Day

Trust in the Lord with all thine heart; and lean not unto thine own understanding. In all thy ways acknowledge Him, and He shall direct thy paths.—Proverbs 3:5-6

Date: Su / M / Tu / W / Th / F / Sa

__ / __ / ____

Today I Feel:

I am thankful for _____ because

_____

_____ .

Blessings the Day Has Brought:

1 _____

2 _____

3 _____

Moment of Reflection

Write about something or someone you love with all your heart.

Date: Su / M / Tu / W / Th / F / Sa

__ / __ / ____

Today I Feel:

I am thankful for _____ because

_____

_____.

Blessings the Day Has Brought:

1 _____

2 _____

3 _____

Bible Verse for the Day

Be strong and courageous. Don't be afraid or scared of them, for ... God Himself is who goes with you. He will not fail you nor forsake you.
—Deuteronomy 31:6

Date: Su / M / Tu / W / Th / F / Sa
__ / __ / ____

Today I Feel:

I am thankful for _____ because

_____

_____ .

Blessings the Day Has Brought:

1 _____

2 _____

3 _____

Moment of Reflection

What did God do for you today?

Date: Su / M / Tu / W / Th / F / Sa

__ / __ / ____

Today I Feel:

I am thankful for _____ because

_____

_____ .

Blessings the Day Has Brought:

1 _____

2 _____

3 _____

Bible Verse for the Day

Cause me to hear your loving kindness in the morning, for I trust in you. Cause me to know the way in which I should walk, for I lift up my soul to you.
—Psalms 143:8

Date: Su / M / Tu / W / Th / F / Sa

__ / __ / ____

Today I Feel:

I am thankful for _____ because

_____

_____ .

Blessings the Day Has Brought:

1 _____
2 _____
3 _____

Moment of Reflection

What did you do today that would make Jesus proud?

Date: Su / M / Tu / W / Th / F / Sa

__ / __ / ____

Today I Feel:

😄 😊 😐 😔 😟

I am thankful for _____ because

_____

_____ .

Blessings the Day Has Brought:

1 _____
2 _____
3 _____

Bible Verse for the Day

Don't you be afraid, for I am with you. Don't be dismayed, for I am your God. I will strengthen you. Yes, I will help you. Yes, I will uphold you with the right hand of my righteousness.—Isaiah 41:10

Date: Su / M / Tu / W / Th / F / Sa

__ / __ / ____

Today I Feel:

I am thankful for _____ because

_____

_____ .

Blessings the Day Has Brought:

1 _____

2 _____

3 _____

Moment of Reflection

Write about a time when you followed God's word.

Date: Su / M / Tu / W / Th / F / Sa
__ / __ / ____

Today I Feel:

I am thankful for _____ because

_____

_____ .

Blessings the Day Has Brought:

1 _____

2 _____

3 _____

Bible Verse for the Day

Your word is a lamp to my feet, and a light for my path.—Psalms 119:105

Date: Su / M / Tu / W / Th / F / Sa

__ / __ / ____

Today I Feel:

I am thankful for _____ because

_____

_____ .

Blessings the Day Has Brought:

1 _____

2 _____

3 _____

Moment of Reflection

Write about a time when God's word guided you.

Date: Su / M / Tu / W / Th / F / Sa
__ / __ / ____

Today I Feel:

I am thankful for _____ because

_____

_____ .

Blessings the Day Has Brought:

1 _____

2 _____

3 _____

Bible Verse for the Day

Be kind to one another, tender hearted, forgiving each other, just as God also in Christ forgave you.
—Ephesians 4:32

Date: Su / M / Tu / W / Th / F / Sa
__ / __ / ____

Today I Feel:

I am thankful for _____ because

_____

_____ .

Blessings the Day Has Brought:

1 _____
2 _____
3 _____

Moment of Reflection

Write about a time you forgave someone and how it felt.

Date: Su / M / Tu / W / Th / F / Sa
__ / __ / ____

Today I Feel:

I am thankful for _____ because

_____

_____ .

Blessings the Day Has Brought:

1 _____

2 _____

3 _____

Bible Verse for the Day

You will keep whoever's mind is steadfast in perfect peace, because they trust in you.—Isaiah 26:3

Date: Su / M / Tu / W / Th / F / Sa
__ / __ / ____

Today I Feel:

I am thankful for _____ because
_____
_____ .

Blessings the Day Has Brought:

1 _____
2 _____
3 _____

Moment of Reflection

What's one thing you are grateful for today?

Date: Su / M / Tu / W / Th / F / Sa
__ / __ / ____

Today I Feel:

I am thankful for _____ because
_____
_____ .

Blessings the Day Has Brought:

1 _____
2 _____
3 _____

Bible Verse for the Day

Set your mind on things that are above, not on things that are on the earth.—Colossians 3:2

Date: Su / M / Tu / W / Th / F / Sa
__ / __ / ____

Today I Feel:

I am thankful for _____ because

_____

_____ .

Blessings the Day Has Brought:

1 _____
2 _____
3 _____

Moment of Reflection

What do you want to pray to God about today?

Date: Su / M / Tu / W / Th / F / Sa
__ / __ / ____

Today I Feel:

I am thankful for _____ because

_____

_____ .

Blessings the Day Has Brought:

1 _____

2 _____

3 _____

Bible Verse for the Day

Rejoicing in hope; enduring in troubles; continuing steadfastly in prayer.—Romans 12:12

Date: Su / M / Tu / W / Th / F / Sa

__ / __ / ____

Today I Feel:

I am thankful for _____ because

_____

_____ .

Blessings the Day Has Brought:

1 _____

2 _____

3 _____

Moment of Reflection

What is something you hope for in the future?

Date: Su / M / Tu / W / Th / F / Sa
__ / __ / ____

Today I Feel:

I am thankful for _____ because

_____

_____ .

Blessings the Day Has Brought:

1 _____

2 _____

3 _____

Bible Verse for the Day

As you would like people to do to you, do exactly so to them.
—Luke 6:31

Date: Su / M / Tu / W / Th / F / Sa
__ / __ / ____

Today I Feel:

I am thankful for _____ because

_____

_____ .

Blessings the Day Has Brought:

1 _____

2 _____

3 _____

Moment of Reflection

What did you do for others today?

Date: Su / M / Tu / W / Th / F / Sa

__ / __ / ____

Today I Feel:

I am thankful for _____ because

_____

_____ .

Blessings the Day Has Brought:

1 _____

2 _____

3 _____

Bible Verse for the Day	But the fruit of the Spirit is love, joy, peace, patience, kindness, goodness, faith, gentleness, and self-control. —Galatians 5:22–23

Date: Su / M / Tu / W / Th / F / Sa

__ / __ / ____

Today I Feel:

I am thankful for _____ because

_____

_____ .

Blessings the Day Has Brought:

1 _____

2 _____

3 _____

Moment of Reflection

What did you do today that Jesus might have done?

Date: Su / M / Tu / W / Th / F / Sa

__ / __ / ____

Today I Feel:

I am thankful for _____ because

_____

_____ .

Blessings the Day Has Brought:

1 _____

2 _____

3 _____

Bible Verse for the Day

The Lord is my shepherd; I shall not want.—Psalms 23:1

Date: Su / M / Tu / W / Th / F / Sa
__ / __ / ____

Today I Feel:

😄 😊 😐 😔 ☹️

I am thankful for _____ because

_____

_____ .

Blessings the Day Has Brought:

1 _____
2 _____
3 _____

Moment of Reflection	How has God guided you?

Date: Su / M / Tu / W / Th / F / Sa
__ / __ / ____

Today I Feel:

I am thankful for _____ because

_____

_____.

Blessings the Day Has Brought:

1 _____
2 _____
3 _____

Bible Verse for the Day	Cast all your worries on Him because He cares for you. —1 Peter 5:7

Date: Su / M / Tu / W / Th / F / Sa
__ / __ / ____

Today I Feel:

I am thankful for _____ because

_____

_____ .

Blessings the Day Has Brought:

1 _____
2 _____
3 _____

Moment of Reflection

How did you care for someone today?

Date: Su / M / Tu / W / Th / F / Sa
__ / __ / ____

Today I Feel:

I am thankful for _____ because

_____

_____ .

Blessings the Day Has Brought:

1 _____

2 _____

3 _____

Bible Verse for the Day	Jesus Christ is the same yesterday, today, and forever.—Hebrews 13:8

Date: Su / M / Tu / W / Th / F / Sa

__ / __ / ____

Today I Feel:

I am thankful for _____ because

_____

_____.

Blessings the Day Has Brought:

1 _____

2 _____

3 _____

Moment of Reflection

How were you like Jesus today?

Date: Su / M / Tu / W / Th / F / Sa
__ / __ / ____

Today I Feel:

😄 🙂 😐 😔 😣

I am thankful for _____ because

_____

_____ .

Blessings the Day Has Brought:

1 _____

2 _____

3 _____

Bible Verse for the Day

You are all children of God, through faith in Christ Jesus. For as many of you as were baptized into Christ have put on Christ.—Galatians 3:26–27

Date: Su / M / Tu / W / Th / F / Sa

__ / __ / ____

Today I Feel:

I am thankful for _____ because

_____

_____ .

Blessings the Day Has Brought:

1 _____

2 _____

3 _____

Moment of Reflection

What does faith mean to you?

Date: Su / M / Tu / W / Th / F / Sa

__ / __ / ____

—— Today I Feel: ——

I am thankful for _____ because

_____

_____ .

Blessings the Day Has Brought:

1 _____

2 _____

3 _____

Bible Verse for the Day	May the God of hope fill you with all joy and peace in believing, that you may abound in hope, in the power of the Holy Spirit.—Romans 15:13

Date: Su / M / Tu / W / Th / F / Sa

__ / __ / ____

Today I Feel:

I am thankful for _____ because

_____

_____.

Blessings the Day Has Brought:

1 _____

2 _____

3 _____

Moment of Reflection

Write about something or someone that brings you joy.

Date: Su / M / Tu / W / Th / F / Sa
__ / __ / ____

Today I Feel:

I am thankful for _____ because

_____

_____ .

Blessings the Day Has Brought:

1 _____

2 _____

3 _____

Bible Verse for the Day

Now the Lord is the Spirit, and where the Spirit of the Lord is, there is liberty.—2 Corinthians 3:17

Date: Su / M / Tu / W / Th / F / Sa
__ / __ / ____

Today I Feel:

I am thankful for _____ because _____
_____.

Blessings the Day Has Brought:

1 _____
2 _____
3 _____

Moment of Reflection

What prayers is God answering in your life?

Date: Su / M / Tu / W / Th / F / Sa

__ / __ / ____

Today I Feel:

I am thankful for _____ because

_____

_____ .

Blessings the Day Has Brought:

1 _____

2 _____

3 _____

Bible Verse for the Day	We know that all things work together for good for those who love God, for those who are called according to His purpose.—Romans 8:28

Date: Su / M / Tu / W / Th / F / Sa

__ / __ / ____

Today I Feel:

I am thankful for _____ because

_____

_____ .

Blessings the Day Has Brought:

1 _____
2 _____
3 _____

Moment of Reflection

Write about some ways you show your love for God.

Date: Su / M / Tu / W / Th / F / Sa
__ / __ / ____

Today I Feel.

I am thankful for _____ because

_____

_____ .

Blessings the Day Has Brought:

1 _____

2 _____

3 _____

Bible Verse for the Day	We know and have believed the love which God has for us. God is love, and he who remains in love remains in God, and God remains in him. —1 John 4:16

Date: Su / M / Tu / W / Th / F / Sa

__ / __ / ____

Today I Feel:

I am thankful for _____ because

_____

_____ .

Blessings the Day Has Brought:

1 _____

2 _____

3 _____

Moment of Reflection

How did you see that you need Jesus today?

Date: Su / M / Tu / W / Th / F / Sa
__ / __ / ____

Today I Feel.

I am thankful for _____ because

_____

_____ .

Blessings the Day Has Brought:

1 _____

2 _____

3 _____

Bible Verse for the Day

It is of the Lord's mercies that we are not consumed, because His compassions fail not. They are new every morning: great is thy faithfulness.—Lamentations 3:22–23

Date: Su / M / Tu / W / Th / F / Sa
__ / __ / ____

Today I Feel:

I am thankful for _____ because

_____

_____.

Blessings the Day Has Brought:

1 _____
2 _____
3 _____

Moment of Reflection

What do you love most about you?

Date: Su / M / Tu / W / Th / F / Sa
__ / __ / ____

Today I Feel:

I am thankful for _____ because

_____

_____ .

Blessings the Day Has Brought:

1 _____
2 _____
3 _____

Bible Verse for the Day

Oh give thanks to God, for He is good, for His loving kindness endures forever.—1 Chronicles 16:34

Date: Su / M / Tu / W / Th / F / Sa

__ / __ / ____

Today I Feel:

😄 😊 😐 😔 😫

I am thankful for _____ because

_____

_____ .

Blessings the Day Has Brought:

1 _____

2 _____

3 _____

Moment of Reflection

What is something you'd like to thank God for today?

Date: Su / M / Tu / W / Th / F / Sa

__ / __ / ____

Today I feel:

I am thankful for _____ because

_____

_____.

Blessings the Day Has Brought:

1 _____

2 _____

3 _____

Bible Verse for the Day	You are the light of the world. A city located on a hill cannot be hidden. —Matthew 5:14

Date: Su / M / Tu / W / Th / F / Sa

__ / __ / ____

Today I Feel:

I am thankful for _____ because

_____

_____ .

Blessings the Day Has Brought:

1 _____

2 _____

3 _____

Moment of Reflection

What is something that makes you special?

Date: Su / M / Tu / W / Th / F / Sa
__ / __ / ____

Today I Feel.

I am thankful for _____ because
_____
_____ .

Blessings the Day Has Brought:

1 _____
2 _____
3 _____

Bible Verse for the Day	May He grant you your heart's desire, and fulfill all your counsel. —Psalms 20:4

Date: Su / M / Tu / W / Th / F / Sa

__ / __ / ____

Today I Feel:

I am thankful for _____ because

_____

_____ .

Blessings the Day Has Brought:

1 _____

2 _____

3 _____

Moment of Reflection

Write about a goal you have and how you plan to achieve it.

Date: Su / M / Tu / W / Th / F / Sa
__ / __ / ____

Today I Feel.

I am thankful for _____ because

_____

_____ .

Blessings the Day Has Brought:

1 _____
2 _____
3 _____

Bible Verse for the Day

Watch! Stand firm in the faith! Be courageous! Be strong! Let all that you do be done in love.
—1 Corinthians 16:13–14

Date: Su / M / Tu / W / Th / F / Sa

__ / __ / ____

Today I Feel:

I am thankful for _____ because

_____

_____ .

Blessings the Day Has Brought:

1 _____

2 _____

3 _____

Moment of Reflection

Write about something or someone you love.

Date: Su / M / Tu / W / Th / F / Sa

__ / __ / ____

Today I feel:

😄 😊 😐 😔 ☹️

I am thankful for _____ because

_____

_____ .

Blessings the Day Has Brought:

1 _____
2 _____
3 _____

Bible Verse for the Day

I can do all things through Christ, who strengthens me.
—Philippians 4:13

Date: Su / M / Tu / W / Th / F / Sa

__ / __ / ____

Today I Feel:

I am thankful for _____ because

_____

_____ .

Blessings the Day Has Brought:

1 _____

2 _____

3 _____

Moment of Reflection

Write about a time you called upon God for strength.

Date: Su / M / Tu / W / Th / F / Sa
__ / __ / ____

Today I feel:

I am thankful for _____ because

_____

_____ .

Blessings the Day Has Brought:

1 _____

2 _____

3 _____

Bible Verse for the Day

What then shall we say about these things? If God is for us, who can be against us?—Romans 8:31

Date: Su / M / Tu / W / Th / F / Sa
__ / __ / ____

Today I Feel:

I am thankful for _____ because

_____

_____ .

Blessings the Day Has Brought:

1 _____
2 _____
3 _____

Moment of Reflection

What or who do you pray for today?

Date: Su / M / Tu / W / Th / F / Sa

__ / __ / ____

Today I feel:

I am thankful for _____ because

_____

_____ .

Blessings the Day Has Brought:

1 _____

2 _____

3 _____

Bible Verse for the Day

A friend loves at all times, and a brother is born for adversity.
—Proverbs 17:17

Date: Su / M / Tu / W / Th / F / Sa
__ / __ / ____

Today I Feel:

I am thankful for _____ because
_____
_____ .

Blessings the Day Has Brought:

1 _____
2 _____
3 _____

Moment of Reflection

How did you help a friend today?

Date: Su / M / Tu / W / Th / F / Sa

__ / __ / ____

Today I feel:

😄 😊 😐 😔 ☹️

I am thankful for _____ because

_____

_____.

Blessings the Day Has Brought:

1 _____

2 _____

3 _____

Bible Verse for the Day

For I . . . your God, will hold your right hand, saying to you, "Don't be afraid. I will help you." —Isaiah 41:13

Date: Su / M / Tu / W / Th / F / Sa

__ / __ / ____

Today I Feel:

I am thankful for _____ because

_____

_____ .

Blessings the Day Has Brought:

1 _____

2 _____

3 _____

Moment of Reflection

How did God show up in your day today?

Date: Su / M / Tu / W / Th / F / Sa

__ / __ / ____

Today I Feel:

I am thankful for _____ because

_____

_____ .

Blessings the Day Has Brought:

1 _____

2 _____

3 _____

Bible Verse for the Day

God is our refuge and strength, a very present help in trouble.
—Psalms 46:1

Date: Su / M / Tu / W / Th / F / Sa

__ / __ / ____

Today I Feel:

I am thankful for _____ because

_____

_____ .

Blessings the Day Has Brought:

1 _____

2 _____

3 _____

Moment of Reflection

What are some things God has blessed you with?

Date: Su / M / Tu / W / Th / F / Sa
__ / __ / ____

Today I Feel:

I am thankful for _____ because

_____

_____ .

Blessings the Day Has Brought:

1 _____
2 _____
3 _____

Bible Verse for the Day

The Lord shall preserve thee from evil: He shall preserve thy soul.
—Psalms 121:7

Date: Su / M / Tu / W / Th / F / Sa
__ / __ / ____

Today I Feel:

I am thankful for _____ because

_____

_____ .

Blessings the Day Has Brought:

1 _____

2 _____

3 _____

Moment of Reflection

Write about a time when God protected you.

Date: Su / M / Tu / W / Th / F / Sa

__ / __ / ____

Today I Feel:

I am thankful for _____ because

_____

_____ .

Blessings the Day Has Brought:

1 _____
2 _____
3 _____

Bible Verse for the Day

The Lord is my rock, and my fortress, and my deliverer; my God, my strength, in whom I will trust; my buckler, and the horn of my salvation, and my high tower.—Psalms 18:2

Date: Su / M / Tu / W / Th / F / Sa

__ / __ / ____

Today I Feel:

I am thankful for _____ because

_____

_____ .

Blessings the Day Has Brought:

1 _____

2 _____

3 _____

Moment of Reflection

How has God helped you today?

Date: Su / M / Tu / W / Th / F / Sa
__ / __ / ____

Today I Feel:

I am thankful for _____ because

_____

_____.

Blessings the Day Has Brought:

1 _____

2 _____

3 _____

Bible Verse for the Day

Come to me, all you who labor and are heavily burdened, and I will give you rest.—Matthew 11:28

Date: Su / M / Tu / W / Th / F / Sa
__ / __ / ____

Today I Feel:

I am thankful for _____ because

_____

_____ .

Blessings the Day Has Brought:

1 _____
2 _____
3 _____

Moment of Reflection

When you're having a bad day, how can God make it better?

THE LORD'S PRAYER
(Matthew 6:9–13)

Our Father which art in heaven, Hallowed be thy name.

Thy kingdom come, Thy will be done in earth, as it is in heaven.

Give us this day our daily bread.

And forgive us our debts, as we forgive our debtors.

And lead us not into temptation, but deliver us from evil: For thine is the kingdom, and the power, and the glory, forever. Amen.

PRAYER FOR SPIRITUAL WISDOM
(Ephesians 1:13–16)

In Him you also, having heard the word of the truth, the Good News of your salvation—in whom, having also believed, you were sealed with the promised Holy Spirit, who is a pledge of our inheritance, to the redemption of God's own possession, to the praise of His glory.

For this cause I also, having heard of the faith in the Lord Jesus which is among you, and the love which you have toward all the saints, don't cease to give thanks for you, making mention of you in my prayers.

A PSALM OF DAVID
(Psalm 30)

I will extol thee, O Lord; for thou hast lifted me up, and hast not made my foes to rejoice over me. . . .

O Lord, thou hast brought up my soul from the grave: thou hast kept me alive, that I should not go down to the pit.

Sing unto the Lord, O ye saints of His, and give thanks at the remembrance of His holiness.

For His anger endureth but a moment; in His favor is life: weeping may endure for a night, but joy cometh in the morning.

And in my prosperity I said, I shall never be moved.

Lord, by thy favor thou hast made my mountain to stand strong; thou didst hide thy face, and I was troubled.

I cried to thee, O Lord; and unto the Lord I made supplication.

What profit is there in my blood, when I go down to the pit? Shall the dust praise thee? Shall it declare thy truth?

Hear, O Lord, and have mercy upon me: Lord, be thou my helper.

Thou hast turned for me my mourning into dancing: thou hast put off my sackcloth, and girded me with gladness;

To the end that my glory may sing praise to thee, and not be silent. O Lord my God, I will give thanks unto thee for ever.

PRAYER FOR SPIRITUAL STRENGTH
(Ephesians 3:14–21)

For this cause, I bow my knees to the
Father of our Lord Jesus Christ, from
whom every family in heaven and on
earth is named, that He would grant you,
according to the riches of His glory, that
you may be strengthened with power
through His Spirit in the inner person,
that Christ may dwell in your hearts
through faith, to the end that you, being
rooted and grounded in love, may be
strengthened to comprehend with all the
saints what is the width and length and
height and depth, and to know Christ's
love which surpasses knowledge, that

you may be filled with all the fullness of God.

Now to Him who is able to do exceedingly abundantly above all that we ask or think, according to the power that works in us, to Him be the glory in the assembly and in Christ Jesus to all generations forever and ever. Amen.